Oh No!

Story by Scharlaine Cairns
Illustrations by Geoff Hocking

 RIGBY

There's a spot on my coat.

There's a spot on my skirt.

There's a spot on my pants
where I fell in the dirt.
Oh No!

There's a spot on my sweater.

There's a spot on my tie.

There's a spot on my chin
from this blueberry pie.
Oh No!

There's a spot on my shorts.

There's a spot on my knee.

9

There's a spot on my dress
everybody can see.
Oh No!

There's a spot on my spoon.

There's a spot on my bowl.

There's a spot on my cup
and it looks like a hole.
Oh No!

13

There's a spot on my hand.

There's a spot on my face.

And now I'm in bed
with spots every place.
OH NO!